Supreme Errors in Judgment:

Money Is Not Speech & A Corporation Is Not A Person

By

E. L. D'Felio

Unus est Populus

TABLE OF CONTENTS

The Supreme Court	4
Judicial Review	11
Living Constitution	14
Constitutional Law	18
The Nature, Origin, and Purpose of Money	22
Buckley v. Valeo	26
The Nature, Origin, and Purpose of Corporations	33
Santa Clara County v. Southern Pacific Railroad	40
First National Bank of Boston v. Bellotti	48
Citizens United v. FEC	56
The More Things Change, The More They Remain The Same	62
Appendix	72

THE SUPREME COURT

"EQUAL JUSTICE UNDER LAW" are the words inscribed in marble on the facade of the edifice of the United States Supreme Court. Those four words encapsulate not only the beliefs and ideals of the Justices, but most importantly, the American people.

Established under Article III, Section 1 of the Constitution and under the authority of the Judiciary Act of September 24, 1789, the Supreme Court is the highest court of law in the United States. As such, the Court is the definitive authority of the law, making it responsible for upholding (the concept of) equal justice under the law, and functioning as guardian and interpreter of the Constitution. [[i]] The Court is the only part of the federal judiciary specifically required by the Constitution. If necessary, the Court also possesses the power to check the actions of the executive branch of the president and the legislative branch of Congress. [[ii]]

As interpreters of the Constitution, Justices have employed a variety of methods of interpretation to support the decisions they have rendered since ratification. The following is a list of elucidations that have been utilized:

- Textualism: Textualism focuses on the plain meaning of the text of a legal document. Textualism emphasizes how the terms in the Constitution would have been understood by people at the time of ratification, as well as the context in which those terms appear. Textualists believe there is an objective meaning of the text, and they do not typically inquire into questions regarding the intent of the drafters, adopters, or ratifiers of the Constitution and its amendments when deriving meaning from the text.

- Original Meaning: Originalist approaches consider the meaning of the Constitution as understood by at least some segment of the populace at the time of ratification. They believe that the Constitution's text had an "objectively identifiable" or public meaning at the time of the founding that has not changed over time, and the task of Justices is to construct this original meaning.
- Judicial Precedent: The utilization of prior Supreme Court decisions for deciding future cases with identical or similar facts, or legal issues.
- Pragmatism: The Court weighs or balances the possible consequences of one interpretation of the Constitution against other interpretations. Another option weighs the future costs and benefits of an interpretation that may lead to the perceived best outcome.
- Moral Reasoning: The contention that specific moral concepts or ideals underlie various

- terms in the Constitution, such as due process of law. The moral or ethical arguments are related to limited government authority over individual rights.
- National Identity (or "Ethos"): Reliance on the belief of a national identity. The distinctive characteristics and values of America define Constitutional meaning.
- Structuralism: The design or structure of the Constitution extracts inferences from the relationships within, such as the executive, judicial, and legislative branches; the federal and state governments; and the government and the people.
- Historical Practices: Like judicial precedents, historical political practices or traditions have served as a source for Constitutional meaning. [[iii]]

The numerous interpretations of the Constitution are the result of an abuse of power, position, and politics within the executive, judicial, and legislative branches of government. In short, the evolution of Constitutional interpretation is the result of political expediency: opting for convenience instead of morality.

Documented history indicates that textualism, original meaning, and judicial precedent are the only acceptable methods of interpretation. Prior to the ratification of the Constitution, colonial courts followed traditional principles of English common law, which included strict interpretation. [[iv]] A concept (English common law) that is still practiced today. Upon his election in 1801, Thomas Jefferson stated:

"The Constitution on which our Union rests, shall be administered by me [as President] according to the safe and honest meaning contemplated by the plain understanding of the people of the United States at the time of its adoption—a meaning to be found in the explanations of those who advocated, not those who opposed it, and who opposed it merely lest the construction should be applied which they denounced as possible." [[v]]

Less than four years after ratification, Jefferson was explicit that textualism and original meaning would be the proper forms of interpretation. In a letter to Thomas Ritchie, James Madison on September 15, 1821, stated that the:

> *"legitimate meaning of the Instrument [Constitution] must be derived from the text itself; or if a key is to be sought elsewhere, it must be not in the opinions or intentions of the Body which planned & proposed the Constitution, but in the sense attached to it by the people in their respective State Conventions where it recd. all the authority which it possesses."*

As "The father of the Constitution," Madison is specifically proclaiming that textualism and original meaning are the only acceptable methods of interpretation. Not to mention he is quite explicit that interpreting the Constitution was never meant to be based upon the "opinions or intentions" of future generations (e.g., Supreme Court Justices), no matter how noble their intent.

Strict interpretation of the Constitution, by default, is an innate precedent derived from centuries of English common law, upon which the legal system in the United States is based.
Similarly, the Supreme Court [often] relies heavily on prior court decisions in formal adjudications. In a common law system, judicial determinations in earlier court cases are extremely critical to the court's resolution of the issue before it.

Proponents of original meaning and textualism point to their long history and commitment to the people who drafted, proposed, adopted, or ratified the Constitution. They contend that if law is to fulfill its objective, it must have a definitive meaning until it is officially amended by Congress and the states. Proponents also assert that originalism and textualism minimize judicial discretion, which prevents judges from rendering decisions based upon their own economic, political, or social views. These approaches ensure more certainty, predictability, and stability in rendering judgments.

Opponents of the original meaning and textualism approaches emphasize the difficulties and inconsistencies in establishing or deciphering "original meaning" of the words or text used by the Founding Fathers and all the other people who participated in the debates at the federal and state levels during the drafting and ratification process. This opinion suggests that a consensus on original meaning is vacant throughout the Constitution, which facilitates the Justices to render decisions based upon their beliefs. Opponents also proclaim that these approaches require the Justices to assume the role of historians as opposed to decision makers. [[vi]]

Apart from original meaning and textualism, prior Supreme Court decisions assist the Justices on constitutional law interpretations in future cases. The advantage of using precedents is that they establish legitimacy to prior decisions; provide predictability to cases with similar circumstances; provide consistency to principles, rules, and standards in rendering judicial decisions; and ensures stability to all parties, including society, who depend upon the Court's decisions.

The disadvantage of precedents comes when a case has been incorrectly determined. Another contention is that precedents render the Court unyielding in adjudicating future cases.

In recent years, the decisions rendered by the Court have called into question its duty and responsibility as guardian and interpreter of the Constitution. This trend should be of no surprise when the Court has failed to follow the original intent of the Founders and the Constitution. The legitimacy of the Court has been jeopardized by partisan politics, legislating from the bench, ignoring precedent, and failing to conduct thorough Constitutional research to name a few. Ironically, the Justices (throughout the Court's history) have no one to blame but themselves; however, they continually fail to recognize their own errors in judgment and place the culpability primarily on outside influences. The net impact on society has been divisiveness and chaos, which has eroded the tenets of the democratic republic.

There are three specific areas that have contributed to the predicament the Court currently finds itself in, and they all pertain to the abuse of power and misinterpreting original intent. They are judicial review, living Constitution, and Constitutional law.

JUDICIAL REVIEW

The power of the Supreme Court to declare an Executive of Legislative act unconstitutional is known as judicial review. Absent from the Constitution itself, the doctrine was established in 1803 in the case of *Marbury v. Madison*. However, like all things political, the events surrounding the *Marbury v. Madison* decision clearly exemplify that the Court has consistently been an active participant in the arena.

To secure a more powerful central government, the Federalists, who controlled Congress and the Presidency, passed the Judiciary Act of 1801 on February 13th, eighteen days before the newly elected president, Thomas Jefferson, took office. The Federalists even voted to reduce the number of Supreme Court seats to five from six when the next vacancy occurred so Jefferson couldn't appoint anyone.

Although Thomas Jefferson was John Adams' Vice-President, the two were political rivals in terms of political ideology and philosophy. The last-ditch efforts of Adams and Congress were as much based on spite for their heavily contested loss to Jefferson as it was to minimize the power of the states, whom they deemed "the corrupters of public opinion."

Prior to the passage of the Judiciary Act,

Adams rushed to fill the vacancy left by the retirement of Chief Justice Oliver Ellsworth. On January 31, 1801, thirty-one days before Jefferson was to take office as President, John Marshall was appointed as Chief Justice. Although they were third cousins, Jefferson and Marshall disliked one another immensely. Jefferson considered Marshall unfit for the judiciary and wrote of his "lax lounging manners." [[vii]] On the contrary, Marshall did not care for Jefferson's failure to serve in the Revolutionary War and suffer the consequences thereof as did Marshall or their contemporaries. [[viii]]

As part of the Judiciary Act of 1801, outgoing President Adams, a staunch Federalist, appointed 16 judges to preside over newly defined court districts. When Jefferson, a Democratic-Republican, took office, his Secretary of State, James Madison, was directed to hold the appointments to Adams' judges. William Marbury, one of the judges, took exception to Madison's compliance and filed an appeal to the Supreme Court.

Marbury sought a writ of mandamus from the Court based upon the Judiciary Act of 1789. However, Chief Justice John Marshall ruled that the section of the Act permitting writs of mandamus directly to the Court by a plaintiff was unconstitutional, and that Congress exceeded its constitutional authority when it passed the Act. [[ix]] The significance of the *Marbury* ruling was that it established the precedent of judicial review: the power of the U.S. Supreme Court to decide whether a law or decision by the legislative or executive branches of federal government, or any court or agency of the state governments is constitutional.

Heralded as a vital component in the separation of powers between the three branches of government, judicial review was nothing more than a coordinated plan to increase control of the federal government over the states via the Supreme Court as evident by the actions of Congress and Adams noted above. Furthermore, in his book entitled 'Without Precedent: Chief Justice John Marshall and His Times,' Joel Richard Paul contends that *Marbury v. Madison* was a "setup" by Marshall himself "to assert the Court's authority against Jefferson at a time when the Supreme Court's very existence as an independent branch of government was threatened." [[x]]

In summation, the doctrine of judicial review was wholeheartedly political.

LIVING CONSTITUTION

The Constitution of the United States is often referred to as a "living" document. The term living is used to describe the belief that the content of the Constitution should be interpreted in response to the changes in society that each new generation confronts. The mantra of "living Constitution" is said to have its origin dating back to a 1927 book entitled The Living Constitution by David A. Strauss. [[xi]]

As visionaries, the Founding Fathers understood and anticipated the necessity for the Constitution to be flexible enough to accommodate the needs of an ever-changing society. That is exactly why Article V, Amendment Process, was incorporated into the Constitution. To the Founders as a whole, the Constitution was not only the supreme Law of the Land per Article VI, Clause II, it was a binding social contract between the people and their government. Their words unequivocally reject the concept of a living constitution in terms of amending original intent via judicial interpretation as compared to the process detailed in Article V. For example, George Washington, James Madison, and Thomas Jefferson respectively stated:

> *"The basis of our political systems is the right of the people to make and to alter their constitutions*

of government. But the Constitution, which at any time exists, till changed by an explicit and authentic act of the whole people, is sacredly obligatory upon all. If in the opinion of the people the distribution or modification of the constitutional powers be in any particular wrong, let it be corrected by an amendment in the way which the Constitution designates."

"The first and governing maxim in the interpretation of a statute is to discover the meaning of those who made it."

"Our peculiar security is in possession of a written Constitution. Let us not make it a blank paper by construction. If it is, then we have no Constitution."

Ironically, it has been Supreme Court Justices of the twentieth century who have significantly hijacked the Founders' original intent of a living constitution with a deceitful rendition thereof. To illustrate, Justices Felix Frankfurter, Stephen Breyer, and Thurgood Marshall, respectively stated:

"The words of the Constitution are so unrestricted by their intrinsic meaning or by their history or by tradition or by prior decisions that they leave the individual Justice free, if indeed they do not compel him, to gather meaning not from reading the Constitution but from reading life."

"This understanding, underlying constitutional interpretation since the New Deal, reflects the

Constitution's demands for structural flexibility sufficient to adapt substantive laws and institutions to rapidly changing social, economic, and technological conditions."

"I cannot accept this invitation [to celebrate the bicentennial of the Constitution], for I do not believe that the meaning of the Constitution was forever at the Philadelphia Convention. To the contrary, the government they devised was defective from the start."

As the [alleged] guardians of the Constitution, such a belief has not only rendered the Constitution illegitimate, but it has also greatly contributed to the chaos and division within society. When the decisions of the Justices do not align with the law or precedents, the fundamental principle of consistency in common law is infringed upon. Lest it be forgotten, the Constitution and the judicial system are based upon English common law. In such a system, the Justices are compelled to adjudicate their decisions as consistently and reasonably possible with prior decisions on the same issue.

The value of the amendment process is that the Constitution [*Law of the Land*] can be adapted to situations that were not contemplated before. If the Court does not follow the law, follow precedent, or force the legislature to amend a proposed law or the Constitution itself, then it will be impossible to conclude what the law is as it will always be susceptible to manipulation.

CONSTITUTIONAL LAW

The politically motivated decision by John Marshall in *Marbury v. Madison*, granted the Supreme Court the sole power to determine the constitutionality of laws. In his decision, he explains:

> *"It is emphatically the province and duty of the Judicial Department [the judicial branch] to say what the law is. Those who apply the rule to particular cases must, of necessity, expound and interpret that rule. If two laws conflict with each other, the Courts must decide on the operation of each."*

Not only did the decision grant the Court judicial review, but it also disrupted the balance of power between the executive, judicial, and legislative branches as originally intended by the Founders. Although the three branches remained separate, they were no longer equal. In addition to their independence and lifetime appointment, the Justices are completely isolated from electorate, which further complicates the issue.

The consequences of *Marbury* are that numerous Justices, like Marshall, have abused their positional power by deliberately disregarding and/or misinterpreting the text and/or intent of the Founders and the people who ratified the

Constitution. As if ordained by divine intervention, many Justices have self-proclaimed themselves to be above the law, or the law itself. In other instances, some Justices have even taken on an oracle like persona.

Take for instance the 2nd Amendment. Many Justices contend that the text and history of the Constitution, and most importantly the means in which citizens fought and won the Revolutionary War, should have no impact or relevancy in guaranteeing every citizen the right to bear arms. Lest we/they forget that governments can be[come] tyrannical (e.g., the Republic of Rome). They also assert that the Founders could not have envisioned the advancement in weapon technology, and therefore would agree with placing tighter restrictions on gun ownership. To illustrate, Justice Warren Burger stated that:

> *"The gun lobby's interpretation of the Second Amendment is one of the greatest pieces of fraud, I repeat the word fraud, on the American People by special interest groups that I have seen in my lifetime."*

> *"The real purpose of the Second Amendment was to ensure that state armies, the militia, would be maintained for the defense of the state. "The very language of the Second Amendment refutes any argument that it was intended to guarantee every citizen an unfettered right to any kind of weapon he or she desires."*

However, if Justice Burger did his due diligence, put his politics aside, and conducted a thorough research on the subject matter, he would have discovered the true intent of the Founders. For example, in 1788, Tench Coxe, delegate for Pennsylvania to the Continental Congress, explained the intent of the 2nd Amendment when he stated:

> *"Who are the militia? Are they not ourselves? Congress have no power to disarm the militia. Their swords and every other terrible implement of the soldier, are the birthright of an American . . . . The unlimited power of the sword is not in the hands of either the federal or state governments, but, where I trust in God it will ever remain, in the hands of the people."*

Furthermore, the notion that the Founders would not have envisioned advances in weaponry is an insult to their intelligence, and the forward-thinking visionaries that they were. Afterall, they studied history and understood that muskets and cannons superseded bows, spears, swords, and the like.

An even more dangerous condition is when members of the judiciary have no regard for the laws as written and make them up as they go. An example is Judge Richard Posner, U.S. Court of Appeals for the Seventh Circuit, explaining how he adjudicated cases. He stated:

> *"I pay very little attention to legal rules, statutes,*

constitutional provisions. A case is just a dispute. The first thing you do is ask yourself — forget about the law — what is a sensible resolution of this dispute?"

Such beliefs are a threat to civilized society. When judges are at liberty to circumvent or ignore the laws, then the judiciary must accept the fact that the citizenry will surely follow their lead and chaos will ensue. Case in point is the current rise in lawlessness and crime across the country.

Regardless of their ideological or philosophical beliefs, every citizen should be concerned when Justices turn their backs on the laws they swore to uphold. Justices are not appointed to like or dislike the laws. They are required to uphold it. Should the Court or its Justices conclude that a contemporary matter is not addressed in the Constitution, specifically or otherwise, then it should either be accepted as a States issue, remanded back to Congress to be reworked, or be proposed to become an amendment.

In conclusion, the Constitution is *the supreme Law of the Land* not a series of guidelines or preferences to base interpretations upon. If that was the Founders intent, the Constitution would read supreme guidelines for Laws of the Land.

THE NATURE, ORIGIN, AND PURPOSE OF MONEY

The phenomenon known as money is an unintended consequence of the synthesis of economic activity between individuals. Regardless of its shape or material (e.g., coins, seashells, or beads), money is an economic unit that functions as a medium of exchange, a measure of value, or a means of payment for goods and services.

Prior to the establishment of money, individuals directly exchanged or traded their goods or services amongst themselves to satisfy their specific needs and wants. This exchange is known as the barter system. The history of bartering dates to 6000 B.C. when Mesopotamian tribes introduced the concept to the Phoenicians. Goods like tea, salt, weapons, and food were exchanged for each other in the absence of money. [[xii]] Barter economies function only when trading partners with mutually beneficial needs meet in the marketplace and agree to a deal. Economists refer to this as a double coincidence of wants—"double" because there are two parties and a "coincidence of wants" because the two parties have mutually beneficial wants that match up perfectly. W.S. Jevons, a 19th-century English economist, coined the term and explained that it is an inherent flaw in bartering: "The first difficulty in barter is to find two persons whose disposable possessions mutually suit each other's wants. There may be many people wanting, and many possessing those things wanted; but to allow of an act of barter there must be a double coincidence, which will rarely happen." [[xiii]]

The pervasive quandary with the barter system is the time consumed between the buyer and seller finding one another with the item(s) that each party wants. If the criterion is not met, the transaction will not take place. This inefficiency led to the creation of money. Economic monetary systems emerged to facilitate the function of buying and selling in the marketplace by eliminating the double coincidence of wants requisite of the barter system.

It is uncertain who invented money, but historians have placed the first use of metal objects to 5,000 B.C. It is believed that the Lydians were the first Western culture to make coins. [[xiv]] Soon after, other countries and civilizations started to mint their own coins with specific values. The use of coins with specific values made it easier to compare values and facilitate exchange by trading money for goods and services.

The earliest forms of money were referred to as commodity money because they were made from materials that possessed value, such as gold and silver. As the world evolved, civilizations shifted from precious metals to paper bills and non-precious metals. Most of the money used throughout the world today is known as fiat money. Its value is determined by the issuing government and being declared legal tender. The U.S. dollar is both fiat money and legal tender.

To succeed in the marketplace, money must be fungible, durable, portable, recognizable, and stable.

Fungible: Units of the money should be of uniform quality so that they are interchangeable with one another.

Durable: The physical characteristics of the money should be durable enough to retain its usefulness in recurring transactions.

Portable: Money should be divisible and easily carried.

Recognizable: The authenticity of money must be easily recognizable to facilitate the exchange and eliminate transaction costs.

Stable: The value placed on money must remain relatively constant otherwise transaction costs will increase.

Such properties guarantee that the benefit of reducing or eliminating the transaction cost of the double coincidence of wants is not offset by other transaction costs associated with a specific good. [[xv]]

The cumulative effect of money in the marketplace is threefold. First, money is a store of value. Ten dollars today, will be ten dollars two years from now. Second, money is a unit of account.

It is a standard measurement that serves as the basis for prices of goods and service. Third, and most importantly, money is a medium of exchange. Throughout the world, money serves as the means of payment for goods and services.[xvi]

    In summation, prior to money, people traded for the goods and services they needed. The inefficiency of the barter system led to the creation of money. Monetary systems were invented to facilitate the function of buying and selling in the marketplace by eliminating the double coincidence of wants. Money is a universally accepted medium, means, or instrument of payment.

BUCKLEY V. VALEO

This chapter will only address the context of the Supreme Court's decision in the case as it pertains to money as (an expression of) speech for political purposes.

On January 2, 1975, a suit was filed in the U.S. District Court for the District of Columbia by Senator James L. Buckley of New York, and Eugene McCarthy, Presidential candidate and former Senator from Minnesota. Joining Buckley were Congressman William A. Steiger of Wisconsin, Mr. Stewart Rawlings Mott (a major contributor to various political committees), the Committee for a Constitutional Presidency-McCarthy '76, the Conservative Party of the State of New York, the New York Civil Liberties Union, the American Conservative Union, Human Events, Inc., Conservative Victory Fund, the Mississippi Republican Party, and the Libertarian Party. The plaintiffs charged that the Federal Election Campaign Act of 1971 (FECA), as amended in 1974, and the Presidential Election Campaign Fund Act., under which the Commission was formed, and the Presidential Election Campaign Fund Act were unconstitutional on several grounds.

The defendants included Francis R. Valeo,

Secretary of the Senate and Ex officio member of the newly formed Federal Election Commission, and the Commission itself. Other appellees included the Clerk of the House of Representatives W. Pat Jennings, the Comptroller General Elmer B. Staats, and the Attorney General.

On January 24, 1975, pursuant to Section 437h(a) of the FECA, the district court certified the constitutional questions in the case to the U.S. Court of Appeals for the District of Columbia Circuit. On August 15, 1976, the appeals court rendered a decision upholding almost all the substantive provisions of the FECA with respect to contributions, expenditures, and disclosure. The court also sustained the constitutionality of the method of appointing the Commission.

On September 19, 1975, the plaintiffs filed an appeal with the Supreme Court. On January 30, 1976, the Supreme Court, in a per curiam opinion, ruled that the expenditure of money was equivalent to speech. In its landmark decision, the court declared that limitations on the use of money for political purposes were a violation of First Amendment protections for free expression since no significant political expression could be made without the expenditure of money. [[xvii]]

The FECA attempted to limit political contributions which included a $1,000 per candidate, per election, ceiling on contributions by individuals and political committees, a $5,000 per candidate, per election, ceiling on contributions by committees that qualify as multicandidate committees, a $25,000 annual ceiling for all contributions by any individual, and limitations on contributions to political party committees. [[xviii]]

The appellants' positions were that the FECA's limitations on the use of money for political purposes were in violation of First Amendment protections. The Supreme Court concurred in part with the appellants' claim, finding that the restrictions on political contributions and expenditures "necessarily reduce[d] the quantity of expression by restricting the number of issues discussed, the depth of the exploration, and the size of the audience reached. This is because virtually every means of communicating ideas in today's mass society requires the expenditure of money." The Court then determined that such restrictions on political speech could only be justified by an overriding governmental interest.[xix]

Furthermore, the Court found that the expenditure ceiling in the FECA imposed "direct and substantial restraints on the quantity of political speech" and invalidated the expenditure limitations as violations of the First Amendment. [[xx]]

Such determinations are not only an error in judgment, but a demonstration of the Court's lack of imagination and understanding of the nature, origin, and purpose of money.

The first, and most significant, error the Court made was equating money to speech. The two are very distinct. In its simplest form, Merriam-

Webster defines money as something generally accepted as a medium of exchange, a measure of value, or a means of payment, whereas speech is defined as the communication or expression of thoughts in spoken words. As thoroughly documented in the chapter entitled "The Nature, Origin, and Purpose of Money," money evolved from the barter system and the Court overlooked the primary purpose or original intent of money. It was invented to facilitate the function of buying and selling goods and services in the marketplace. Money is a universally accepted medium, means, or instrument of payment. Money can pay for speech in the spoken, printed, or written word, but it (money) is not speech. It simply facilitates the purchasing of speech.

Second, the Court contended that no significant political expression could be made without the expenditure of money. However, data from the 2016 Presidential Election (primaries and national) contradicts said claim. According to mediaQuant, a firm that tracked free media coverage for each candidate and assigned a dollar value based on advertising rates, Donald Trump received $1.898 billion in earned media as compared to Hillary Clinton's $746 million.[xxi] Earned media is news and commentary on television, in newspapers and magazines, and on social media. [[xxii]] Not to mention that presidential candidates are eligible to receive federal funds under the presidential public funding program to pay for the qualified expenses of their political campaigns in both the primary and general elections. [[xxiii]]

Third, the Court's failure to identify an overriding governmental interest in placing restrictions on political speech can only be described as arrogant ignorance. Historical evidence from the presidential election of 1828 to present day points to rewarding political loyalists for their monetary donations. Such rewards have consisted of federal positions (e.g., cabinet secretaries and ambassadorships), influencing political and economic policies or programs, and the like. For example, President Trump selected WWE co-founder Linda McMahon to be administrator of the Small Business Administration after she contributed $7.5 million to his campaign. [[xxiv]] Or President Obama putting Vice President of Level 3 Communications Donald H. Gips in charge of hiring in the White House, and then naming him as ambassador of South Africa after he contributed $500,000 to the Obama campaign. [[xxv]] Coincidently, Level 3 Communications, in which Gips still had stock, later received millions of dollars in government broadband projects though he denied any knowledge. [[xxvi]] Not to mention that a 2011 investigation conducted by iWatch News reported that 200 of Obama's biggest donors had obtained coveted government jobs and advisory posts, won federal contracts worth millions of dollars for their business interests, or attended influential White House meetings and social events.

[[xxvii]]
The conventional wisdom amongst those individuals who have a dependency upon or a personal stake in the political arena contends that campaign contributions are not a form of bribery or an influence of corruption. The common proclamations are that there is no causal relationship or evidence that campaign contributions change the behavior of politicians or that contributions are not a form of bribery influence-peddling. [[xxviii]] As long as money is considered speech, those fallacies will endure.

In conclusion, the erroneous determination by the Court that money equates to speech legitimized bribery in the political process. Money is the instrument that facilitates the buying and selling of speech in the (political) marketplace. The evidence of donors, donations, and political "rewards" noted above is just a minuscule sample of what has transpired throughout history. Legally, bribery is the offering, giving, soliciting, or receiving an item of value to influence the actions of an individual holding a public or legal duty. [[xxix]] Money purchases speech, candidate appoints donor, and bribery is committed.

It is inconceivable, yet not unsurprising given the relationships between the parties involved, that the legal system has failed to comprehend this and the negative consequences it has had on a government of *We the People*. The relevancy or frequency of the donation (bribe) is, and should have always been, irrelevant.

It is also evident by the data noted above that the everyday citizen, who can only afford a campaign donation of $100.00, is not treated in the same manner as a Linda McMahon or Donald H. Gips. Where are the equal protections for the everyday citizens, who comprise ninety-plus percent of the population, but cannot afford extremely large monetary contributions? Are such monetary distinctions irrelevant to legitimate governmental objectives? Isn't a donation a donation regardless of the amount or who made the contribution? Systemically, and in conjunction with their error equating money to speech, the Court also has failed to consider a (possible) connection between the Fifth Amendment's Due Process Clause requiring the United States government to practice equal protection, and the Fourteenth Amendment's Equal Protection Clause requiring states to practice equal protection.

THE NATURE, ORIGIN, AND PURPOSE OF CORPORATIONS

A corporation is an independent legal entity that is organized under state laws. Ownership in a corporation is obtained through the purchase of stock or shares. The principal advantage of a corporation over a sole proprietorship or partnership is complete independence from the stock or shareholders' personal assets. Thus, shareholders are only liable for their investment. The corporate entity serves as a shield from any further liability, which protects their personal assets (e.g., personal bank accounts and properties). [[xxx]] Whereas in sole proprietorships and partnerships the owners are responsible for the company's debts. The preponderance of corporate law happens at the state level. State laws generally outline the duties of corporate officers, shareholder voting processes, procedures for amending bylaws, and the like for proper corporate oversight.

The word 'corporation' comes from the Latin word 'corporare,' which means "to combine in one body." The Romans were the first to organize an entity apart from ownership. The first corporations chartered in Europe were not business corporations. They were religious, municipal, and charitable corporations. It wasn't until the 17th century that making money became a primary focus for corporations.

One of the earliest cases in establishing corporate law was decided in 1613 in England. In Sutton's Hospital, Edward Coke, then Chief Justice of the Common Pleas, concluded that an entity (hospital) "in expectancy or intendment, or nomination" can be a corporation even if its existence is just a thought. Coke further elaborated that corporations were legal constructs and as such, they were not human. He explained:

". . . a corporation aggregate of many is invisible, immortal, and rests only in intendment and consideration of the law. They may not commit treason, nor be outlawed, nor excommunicate, for they have no souls, neither can they appear in person, but by attorney. A corporation aggregate of many cannot do fealty, for an invisible body can neither be in person, nor swear, it is not subject to imbecilities, death of the natural body, and diverse other cases."

William Blackstone, whose Commentaries on the Laws of England have influenced American lawmakers and jurists from the Declaration of Independence to the present day, said this regarding corporations:

"For a corporation, being an invisible body, cannot manifest its intentions by any personal act or oral discourse; . . . It can neither maintain, or be made defendant, to, an action of battery or such like

personal injuries; ... A corporation cannot commit treason, or felony, or other crime, in its corporate capacity: though its members may, in their distinct individual capacities. Neither is it capable of suffering a traitor's, or felon's punishment, for it is not liable to corporal penalties, nor to attainder, forfeiture, or corruption of blood."

The earliest forms of corporations within the thirteen American colonies originated in England. Unlike corporations of today, they required a grant from the Crown and were mainly for commerce or land grants. For example, in the East India Company investors pooled capital into "joint-stock" company from which profits would be distributed according to capital invested. [[xxxi]] Another example is the Virginia Company, which helped expand British control in North America. [[xxxii]] Interestingly, the Virginia Company established the first legislature, the General Assembly, in North America. [[xxxiii]]

After the Revolutionary War, the colonies chose to integrate the corporations that were established under English rule rather than terminating their charters. After Independence, state legislatures, who now had the power to incorporate as compared to the prerogative of the Crown, began forming corporations. These "newly" formed corporations resembled those previously under English rule. They were created for specific public needs, with their charters lasting ten to forty years. A control to minimize corporate misconduct.

Limits were also set on commercial interests, and they were prohibited from participating in the political process. It was not until the 1790s that for-profit corporations started to appear in the United States. For the period covering 1790 to 1860, states chartered 22,419 business corporations under special legislative acts and several thousand more under general incorporation laws that were introduced mostly in the 1840s and 1850s. [[xxxiv]]

The Founding Fathers understood the legality of incorporation. Of the fifty-five delegates who attended the Constitutional Convention, thirty-five of them were attorneys or had received legal training. With their experiences under English rule, they were also aware of the potential dangers of corporations in terms of concentrating economic and political power. This concern was expressed by Thomas Jefferson and James Madison in 1816 and 1827, respectively. They stated:

> *"I hope we shall crush in its birth the aristocracy of our moneyed corporations, which dare already to challenge our government to a trial of strength and bid defiance to the laws of our country."*

> *"Incorporated companies with proper limitations and guards may, in particular cases, be useful; but they are at best a necessary evil only."*

Throughout the years, other presidents echoed similar sentiments. In an 1833 message to Congress, Andrew Jackson asked whether the American people were to govern through their elected representatives or "whether the money and power of a great corporation are to be secretly exerted to influence their judgment and control their decisions." [[xxxv]] In an 1837 message to Congress, President Martin Van Buren warned of:

"the already overgrown influence of corporate authorities." [[xxxvi]]

In an 1888 message to Congress, President Grover Cleveland said:

"Corporations, which should be the carefully restrained creatures of the law and the servants of the people, are fast becoming the people's masters." [[xxxvii]]

Circa 1875, states began to allow corporations to remain in perpetuity as they (the states) competed with one another for corporate charters. [[xxxviii]]

A momentous change in corporate law came in 1886 when the Supreme Court (erroneously) granted corporations the same rights as citizens under the 14th Amendment's Equal Protection Clause in *Santa Clara County v. Southern Pacific Railroad*.

Also, during the 1800s, there was a loosening of strict legislative constraints on corporate charters. For example, in 1896 New Jersey passed a statute that permitted corporations to define the scope of their charters themselves, independent of the government. [[xxxix]] As feared by the Founding

Fathers, many corporations became malicious. In the 1880s, Standard Oil sought to monopolize the oil industry by using unethical measures to eliminate competition. [[xl]] A trial was held in 1908 in which the government produced evidence that the Standard Oil Trust secured illegal railroad discounts, blocked competitors from using oil pipelines, spied on other companies, and bribed elected officials.

The federal government responded to such actions by passing legislation and through the courts. Such actions included the Sherman Antitrust Act of 1890, which sought to limit large corporations' ability to fix prices and exclude competition; Northern Securities Company v. United States that resulted in a 5-4 decision where the Supreme Court ordered the dissolution of J.P. Morgan's Northern Securities Trust; Dodge v. Ford Motor where Henry Ford opted to not pay dividends to shareholders in an attempt "to employ still more men, to spread the benefits of this industrial system to the greatest possible number, [and] to help them build up their lives and their homes;" and, the Securities Exchange Act of 1934, which promoted transparency of public securities by requiring disclosure of audited financial records and empowered the Securities and Exchange Commission to enforce compliance. [[xli]]

The Stock Market Crash of 1929 and the Great Depression produced a shift in the attitudes of the public toward corporations. The triumph of World War II generated another turning point for corporations as they regained the faith of the American people for their contributions to the war effort.

Up through the early 1970s, corporations' goals were the manufacturing of good products, customer satisfaction, good public relations, and a positive return on a shareholder's investment. From the mid-1970s throughout the 1980s, corporations saw a rebirth of laissez-faire capitalism and globalization. Since then, there have been two significant changes. First, a shift from shareholder interests to an emphasis on shareholder value. Second, and most impactful on society, the mobilization of corporate resources to control politics and the courts. [[xlii]]

SANTA CLARA COUNTY V. SOUTHERN PACIFIC RAILROAD

This chapter will only address the absence of corporate personhood and the 14th Amendment in the Court's opinion, while peculiarly granting the railroad constitutional protections.

Prior to 1879, Southern Pacific Railroad was given grants by Congress to facilitate the construction of connecting lines with other interstate railways. In 1879, California's constitution was adopted, which included tax-exempt status on any property owned by either the government of the United States, the state of California, or any county or municipal entities created by the state. [[xliii]] This privilege, however, was not extended to the railroads. Southern Pacific refused to pay the taxes assessed to its charter, roadways, roadbeds, fences, and rolling stock by the California Board of Equalization. [[xliv]] In response, San Mateo County and other adjacent counties brought an action against the railroad to recoup the loss in tax revenue.

The federal district court ruled that the tax assessment was null and void due to lack of the Board's jurisdiction, and ruled that Sothern Pacific was denied equal protection of the law because the assessment wasn't discounted at the rate of the other property owners. San Mateo county filed a writ of error to the federal district, and the Supreme Court heard the case. [[xlv]] Hereafter the case was collectively referred to as *Southern Pacific*.

After hearing the case, the Court concluded that the Board had no authority to assess the taxes. The Court affirmed the judgment for Southern Pacific.

What is most important to note is the fact that the Court's opinion on the case never hints at, mentions, or references corporate personhood or the 14th Amendment. Yet strangely, a headnote written by Reporter of Decisions, John Chandler Bancroft Davis, regarding equal protection of the 14th Amendment found its way into the record. Headnotes are summaries of the issues in the case and are located at the beginning of each opinion to assist the reader in identifying issues within the case. [[xlvi]] In 1906, the Court ruled in *United States v. Detroit Timber & Lumber Co.* that headnotes have no legal standing and therefore do not set precedent.

During his briefing of counsel, Silas Woodruff Sanderson for Southern Pacific, argued that "corporations are persons within the meaning of the Fourteenth Amendment to the Constitution of the United States" and should be entitled to the same right of equal protection under the law. [[xlvii]] Sanderson's assertion was that since the railroad corporation was a person, San Mateo and the other counties couldn't discriminate against it by having different laws and taxes. [[xlviii]] It has also been alleged that during arguments, Justice Waite advised Sanderson to get beyond his assertions that corporations are persons and get to the point of the case: taxation. [[xlix]]

In addition, lead attorney for Southern Pacific, Roscoe Conkling, advised the Court that while a congressman he had worked on the committee drafting the 14th Amendment and that "citizens" had been replaced with "persons" so that corporations would be included.[l] He produced a journal to support his claim. Years later, it was revealed that the journal was authentic, but his account of the events was a lie. [[li]]

In his rebuttal, Delphin Michael Delmas for the counties surmised the absurdities of Southern Pacific's claim when he read aloud a quote from William Blackstone's Commentaries on the Laws of England: [[lii]]

> *"Persons are divided by the law into either natural persons or artificial. Natural persons are such as the God of nature formed us; artificial are such as are created and devised by human laws for the purposes of society and government, which are called corporations or bodies politic."*

For seventeen months the Court deliberated the issue and on May 10, 1886, the decision was rendered. However, prior to the reading, Justice Morrison Waite proclaimed:

"The court does not wish to hear argument on the

question whether the provision in the Fourteenth Amendment to the Constitution, which forbids a state to deny to any person within its jurisdiction the equal protection of the laws, applies to these corporations. We are of the opinion that it does."

Interestingly, and without explanation, the court reporter added a headnote that read:

"The defendant corporations are persons within the intent of the clause in section 1 of the Fourteenth Amendment to the Constitution of the United States, which forbids a State to deny to any person within its jurisdiction the equal protection of the laws."

The remarks contained in the headnote were never spoken by the justices nor were they part of the Court's opinion in the case. The Court never addressed the issue of whether corporations are natural or artificial persons.

From its onset, this case was filled with conflicting and controversial realities that range from ignoring legal doctrine to conflicts of interest. All of which strongly suggest that it be revisited and overturned. The first place to start would be the railroad and its political affiliations in the matter at hand.

The administration of Ulysses S. Grant was plagued with scandals. In 1867 a shell company name Crédit Mobilier of America was formed by stockholders in the Union Pacific Railroad to build the railroad. Shares were then sold or given to influential members of congress who approved subsidies for the project, which garnered large profits. [[liii]] The scandal became public in 1872.

Chief Justice Waite was nominated by Grant on January 19, 1874. Waite had worked with Bancroft Davis in congress and the Alabama Tribunal in Geneva, Switzerland in 1871. [[liv]]

Bancroft Davis, who inserted the infamous headnote, was at one time Grant's Acting Secretary of State. In addition, in 1868 he was elected President of the Board of Directors of the Newburgh and New York Railroad Company. [[lv]]

Not only did Roscoe Conkling commit perjury regarding the alleged change in wording of the 14th Amendment, but he was also nominated twice to the Supreme Court. First as Chief Justice in 1873 and then as an Associate Justice in 1882. He was confirmed by the Senate but decided not to serve.

Although not addressed in the Court's opinion, the issue of whether corporations are citizens or natural persons should have been irrelevant. Per the legal doctrine of stare decisis, corporate personhood was decided in 1819. In *Dartmouth College v. Woodward*, Chief Justice John Marshall wrote that by establishing a corporation, Eleazar Wheelock had created:

> *"an artificial being, invisible, intangible, and existing only in contemplation of the law. Being the mere creature of law, it possesses only those properties which the charter of its creation confers*

upon it."

In 1839, Chief Justice Roger Taney stated in Bank of Augusta v. Earle:

"A corporation can have no legal existence out of the boundaries of the sovereignty by which it is created. It exists only in contemplation of law and by force of the law. ... It is indeed a mere artificial being."

Marshall's and Taney's comments fall in line with the treatises of Edward Coke and William Blackstone:

"a corporation aggregate of many is invisible, immortal, and rests only in intendment and consideration of the law" and *"A corporation cannot commit treason, or felony, or other crime, in its corporate capacity."* [[lvi]]

It is unfathomable how a Supreme Court decision that does not mention corporate personhood became a precedent thereof, overturning a sixty-seven-year-old decision. Evidence suggests and supports that there were no new circumstances or considerable changes in society to justify the Court's actions.

As it pertains to corporate personhood, the Court's history can best be described as an ongoing contradiction of chaos. In 1819, the Contract Clause (Article I, Section 10 declares that No state shall pass any Law impairing the obligation of contracts) was upheld in *Dartmouth College* (a corporation).

Upholding a contract is a far cry from the classification of a person: artificial or natural.

To the contrary of *Southern Pacific* (proclamation of corporate personhood), the Court has repeatedly declined to extend the rights of natural persons to corporations under the Privileges and Immunities Clause of Article IV. Also known as the Comity Clause, the Court in *Bank of Augusta v. Earle* (1839) held that corporations are not covered under the Clause. The Court concluded that;

> *"[t]he only rights [a corporation] can claim are the rights which are given to it in that character, and not the rights which belong to its members as citizens of a state."* [[lvii]]

In conclusion, the Constitution does not mention corporations. This alone renders corporations as an issue for the States to address. The original intent of the 14th Amendment was to grant citizenship rights to African Americans. Between 1886 and 1910, there were 307 Fourteenth Amendment Supreme Court cases: 288 were filed by corporations seeking personhood, while 19 pertained to African Americans. [[lviii]] Although corporations were (erroneously) granted rights under the Equal Protection Clause, they (corporations) do not have identical rights, nor are they treated the same as natural persons. For example, corporations and people are taxed at different rates. The Court's opinion in *Southern Pacific* is vacant on the issue of corporate personhood. Ultimately, the Court's ruling, and the repercussions forwarding, are contrary to Common Law and legal precedent. In addition, and given the association and relationships between Grant's scandals: Justice Waite's appointment and prior work with Bancroft Davis; Roscoe Conkling's fabrication; and Davis's history with Grant and as a former director of a railroad, clearly *Southern Pacific* should be revisited and overturned due to an act of perjury and appearances of partiality by Waite and Davis in carrying out their official duties.

FIRST NATIONAL BANK OF BOSTON V. BELLOTTI

In 1976, Massachusetts amended the 1974 Federal Election Campaign Act, via General Laws Chapter 55 Section 8, to prohibit corporate funds from purchasing advertising to influence the outcome of referendum elections, unless the corporation's business interests were directly involved. [[lix]]

Within the same year, a constitutional amendment was proposed to modify the income tax code by way of a referendum. First National Bank of Boston, New England Merchants National Bank, the Gillette Co., Digital Equipment Corp., and Wyman-Gordon proclaimed that this amendment affected their business interests, thus allowing them to spend corporate funds on relevant advertising. The Massachusetts Attorney General, Francis Bellotti, disagreed. [[lx]] Hereafter the case is collectively referred to as *First National Bank of Boston*.

In response, in April 1976, the corporations filed a suit against Bellotti asserting that Chapter 55 Section 8 was unconstitutional because it violated their First Amendment rights to freedom of speech. In September 1976, the Massachusetts Supreme Court ruled in favor of Bellotti [[lxi]]. First National Bank of Boston filed an appeal to the United States

Supreme Court.

On April 26, 1978, the Supreme Court issued its opinion in *First National Bank of Boston v. Bellotti*. The Court overturned the Massachusetts Supreme Court decision that Chapter 55 Section 8 was constitutional. [[lxii]] On the merits of the case, the Court maintained that Section "8 abridged the expression that the First Amendment was meant to protect." [[lxiii]] In addition, the Court also struck down the law's ban against corporate discussion of ballot measures concerning personal income taxes. The Justices stated that "The legislature is constitutionally disqualified from dictating the subjects about which persons may speak and the speakers who may address a public issue." [[lxiv]]

The justifications for the restrictions in Section 8, "sustaining the active role of the individual citizen in the electoral process and thereby preventing diminution of the citizen's confidence in government" and "protecting the rights of shareholders whose views differ from those expressed by management on behalf of the corporation," were held to be unconstitutional, lacking a persuasive state interest to support the regulation. [[lxv]] The Court asserted that "The risk of corruption perceived in cases involving candidate elections...simply is not present in a popular vote on a public issue," while the contention that Section 8 protected shareholders with differing views was disproven. [[lxvi]] However, the regulation was so restrictive that it prevented corporate expenditures on a referendum even if there was unanimous consent from the shareholders.

Like the decision in *Santa Clara County v. Southern Pacific Railroad*, the Court, in this case, ignored the doctrine of stare decisis and erroneously equated a corporation to a natural person. As previously noted, Edward Coke (in 1613), William Blackstone (in 1765), Justice Marshall (in 1819), and Justice Taney (1839) all concluded that corporations were invisible and immortal: not human. Therefore, based upon stare decisis, the issue of corporate personhood was decided by the Court as early as 1819. To reiterate an earlier point, corporations are not, never have been, nor should they ever be identified as, or equated to citizens or persons. Furthermore, the issue of corporate expenditures for advertising their views on the proposed income tax and shareholder positions that differed from the corporation would be moot.

Regarding the corporations' advertisements, the Court's majority proclaimed that "It is the type of speech indispensable to decision-making in a democracy, and this is no less true because the speech comes from a corporation rather than an individual. The inherent worth of the speech in terms of its capacity for informing the public does not depend on the identity of its source." [[lxvii]] The Court also contended that business communications are a form of expression and entitled to protection to assure the free flow of ideas and information to the public at large. As it pertained to Section 8's prohibition to corporate discussions of ballot measures, the Court said that "the legislature is constitutionally disqualified from dictating the subjects about which persons may speak and the speakers who may address a public issue." [[lxviii]]

In rendering his opinion, Chief Justice Burger incorporates the Press Clause to remove any doubt that may have existed between the original meaning of freedom of speech and freedom of the press. Ironically, and to support his position, Justice Burger does not cite the Founding Fathers, but turns to a newspaperman, Andrew Bradford. The quandary is not "a Liberty, within the Bounds of Law, for any Man, to communicate to the Public, his Sentiments on the Important Points of Religion and Government; of proposing any Laws, which he apprehends may be for the Good of his Country, and of applying for the Repeal of such, as he Judges pernicious ..." but the distinction between the "institutional press" and the printing press itself. [[lxix]] This error in judgement by Burger is akin to that of corporate personhood. It is not the method or process of the speech (e.g., oration or pamphlet), but who delivers the speech: a natural person or an invisible and immortal abstract. To further embellish his position, Burger attempts to equate restricting the speech of inanimate objects, who are incapable of speaking, to that of the licensing system of Tudor and Stuart England.

The fundamental error in judgment by the

Court, in this case, is the notion that speech, which is "indispensable to decision-making in a democracy" has been excluded from being disseminated to the public. Such a contention is nothing more than a legal sleight of hand. As Edward Coke said, a corporation "cannot appear in person ... be beaten ... commit treason ... though its members may, in their distinct individual capacities." [[lxx]] In short, nothing in Section 8, or in the First Amendment, has ever prevented an employee or shareholder of a corporation from speaking on their own behalf, because a corporation, being invisible and immortal, is incapable of any form of speech. The latter is the legal precedent that the Court failed to uphold.

The Court's decision permits corporate officers to don a cloak of invisibility to utilize the financial clout and influence of the entity devoid of personal accountability, expenditures, and responsibilities. The majority also contends that such power in government to monitor and regulate the expression of views is unacceptable under the First Amendment, yet it is simultaneously conveying that such power and influence wielded by corporations, as compared to an individual (natural) citizen, is completely and totally acceptable.

In dissent, Justices White, Brennan, and Marshall correctly identify corporations as "artificial entities created by law for the purpose of furthering certain economic goals." [[lxxi]] In addition, Justice Rehnquist references two decisions in which the Court addresses limitations placed upon corporations. In *Northwestern National Life Insurance Company v. Riggs*, the Court decided that the liberty protected by the First Amendment "is the liberty of natural, not artificial persons," [[lxxii]] while in *United States v. White*, he points out that "the mere creation of a corporation does not invest it with all the liberties enjoyed by natural persons (e.g., corporations do not enjoy the privilege against self-incrimination)." [[lxxiii]] Unfortunately, there is no reference that the minority attempted to invoke the doctrine of stare decisis to revisit and overturn *Southern Pacific Railroad* and the fallacy of corporate personhood.

Furthermore, the dissenting opinion illustrates the (repetitive) historical hypocrisy of the Court. For example, the Corrupt Practices Act of 1907 has prohibited corporate contributions in connection with federal elections. In *United States v. Automobile Workers*, *Pipefitters v. United States*, and *United States v. CIO*, the Court recognized that a principal purpose of the prohibition is "to avoid the deleterious influences on federal elections resulting from the use of money by those who exercise control over large aggregations of capital." [[lxxiv]]

Similarly, in *Abood v. Detroit Board of Education*, the Court declared that a public employee's union could not compel employees to contribute to sociopolitical causes they dispute as a condition of employment because it "impermissibly infringed their First Amendment right to adhere to their own beliefs and to refuse to defer to or support the beliefs of others." [[lxxv]] Forcing shareholders to contribute to causes they disagree with is no different.

In conclusion, the formation and regulation of business entities (e.g., corporations, partnerships, and sole proprietorships) in the United States is a matter of state law. The formation of such entities is not a right, but an honor and privilege. Unlike a partnership or sole proprietorship, corporations enjoy unique regulations such as limited liability, perpetual life, and taxation of assets to promote their economic growth and development. Thus, states have fostered an environment conducive to corporate growth, while simultaneously enriching society. As a result of such a favorable status, corporations possess an enormous amount of economic power, which has translated into political power. Such power wielded by corporations has shifted the balance of the political playing field, which has jeopardized the electoral process and the heart and soul of our democratic republic.

As previously noted, corporations are not (natural) citizens or persons, therefore they are not entitled to the same First Amendment protections. As Abraham Lincoln eloquently stated on November 19, 1863, in his Gettysburg Address, this is a "government of the people, by the people and for the people." Not a government of corporations, by corporations, and for corporations. Lest we forget that corporations aren't even mentioned in the

Constitution. Given its inability to speak, there has never been an impediment to prevent employees and shareholders from expressing or financially supporting their own political causes. Conversely, corporate communications vital to daily business operations are permissible provided they follow the policies and procedures specified in their by-laws and charters.

Government regulations, whether intentional or not, have provided corporations with protections that individual citizens do not enjoy (e.g., tax breaks). Their wealth alone finances political candidates and campaigns, which exerts an undue influence on an election. Appointments to ambassadorships and cabinet positions are enough direct evidence to support this fact.

Paradoxically, the Court has raised the issue of the Fifth Amendment's Due Process Clause and the Fourteenth Amendment's Equal Protection Clause as means of supporting their decisions regarding corporate personhood, yet it has miraculously failed to recognize that said rulings have denied (natural) citizens equal protection under the law. Only by overturning this case (*First National Bank of Boston*) and other similar cases (e.g., *Southern Pacific Railroad* and *Citizens United*) can the balance of the electoral process be restored to the original intent of "one person, one vote."

CITIZENS UNITED V. FEC

This chapter will only address the context of the Supreme Court's decision in the case as it pertains to stare decisis.

In January 2008, Citizens United, a non-profit corporation, released a film about Senator Hillary Clinton, who was a candidate in the Democratic Party's 2008 Presidential primary election. Citizens United wanted to pay cable companies to make the film available for free. Citizens United planned to make the film available within 30 days of the 2008 primary elections but they were concerned that the film would be covered by the Federal Election Campaign Act's ban on corporate-funded electioneering communications that are the functional equivalent of express advocacy, thus subjecting the corporation to civil and criminal penalties. Citizens United sought relief against the Federal Election Commission contending that the ban on corporate electioneering communications and that disclosure and disclaimer requirements were unconstitutional.

On January 21, 2010, the Supreme Court issued a ruling in *Citizens United v. Federal Election Commission* overruling an earlier decision, *Austin v. Michigan State Chamber of Commerce*, which had allowed prohibitions on independent expenditures by corporations.

The majority's opinion stems from the belief that corporations are people, and because of such a belief, they (corporations) are entitled to freely exercise their First Amendment rights to the freedom of speech, or of the press. The Court's belief was so intense that it felt compelled to revisit and overrule *Austin v. Michigan State Chamber of Commerce* and partially overrule *McConnel v. Federal Election Commission*.

On March 27, 1990, the Supreme Court ruled that a Michigan state law prohibiting corporate independent expenditures that opposed or supported any candidate for state office was constitutional. [[lxxvi]] A violation of said law was punishable as a felony. The Court identified anti-distortion as a means of restricting political speech. In Austin, governmental interest in the enormous accumulations of money from corporations was accepted as "corrosive and distorting," while having "little or no correlation to the public's support for the corporation's political ideas." [[lxxvii]]

On December 10, 2003, the Supreme Court declared that prohibitions of soft money under the Federal Election Campaign Act of 1971 and as amended by the Bipartisan Campaign Reform Act of 2002 were necessary to prevent real and obvious acts of corruption of federal candidates and elected officials. [[lxxviii]] The Court also concluded that soft money restrictions on state and local party committees were necessary to thwart those committees from being a channel for soft money. [[lxxix]]

In the second paragraph of his opening statement for the majority in *Citizens United*, Chief Justice Roberts asserts that "Austin was a significant departure from ancient First Amendment principles." [[lxxx]] It is uncertain which ancient principles he was alluding to. However, documented history proves that the Court, past and present, has routinely and intentionally misapplied and misinterpreted whom the First Amendment was written for: animate or inanimate objects.

Throughout the remainder of his opinion, Justice Roberts makes a scientific error of equating corporations with human beings (e.g., citizens or persons). This error is a constant in every position throughout the opinions of the Court. He proclaims that the Court rejects the theory that the rights in the First Amendment are confined to individuals. [[lxxxi]] He further elaborates that the "First Amendment protects more than just the individual on a soapbox and the lonely pamphleteer." [[lxxxii]]

It should be noted that *Citizens United v. FEC* was not the first case in which the Court concluded that corporations are persons or citizens and therefore entitled to the rights established under the First Amendment. Corporate personhood was (erroneously and suspiciously) first established in 1886 in *Santa Clara County v. Southern Pacific Railroad*. Ironically, the Court's ruling and opinion in said case does not even mention the issue of corporate personhood, because the case was a matter of taxation. From *Santa Clara* forward, justices on the Court have routinely ignored Common Law and Supreme Court precedents in pursuit of their own self-interests (e.g., fame, fortune, and power) and ideology. Even the so-called originalists are guilty of ignoring the Founding Fathers' original intent. As previously noted, Edward Coke, William Blackstone, John Marshall, and Roger Taney all proclaimed that corporations are artificial, invisible, and just a thought.

In rendering the Court's opinion, Justice Kennedy proclaims that "stare decisis does not compel the continued acceptance of Austin." [[lxxxiii]] Given the history of the Court's citations of William Blackstone and predominating opinions (e.g., Justices Marshal and Brandeis) that corporations are not citizens or persons, it is quite baffling that the majority opinion failed to revisit, reconsider, and overturn the erroneous repercussions of *Santa Clara* via stare decisis. *Citizens United* is one of several similar cases that demonstrates that the Court has a selective application of the law. If utilized as intended, the doctrine of stare decisis states that the Court will adhere to precedent in rendering their decisions (i.e., "to stand by things decided"). [[lxxxiv]] As previously noted, Edward Coke (in 1613), William Blackstone (in 1765), Justice Marshall (in 1819), and

Justice Taney (1839) all concluded that corporations were invisible and immortal: not human. Therefore, based upon stare decisis, the issue of corporate personhood was decided by the Court as early as 1819. Simply stated, corporations are not, never have been, nor should they ever be identified as, or equated to citizens or persons.

Furthermore, if the Court truly accepted and respected the doctrine of stare decisis after *Dartmouth College* in 1819, then *Santa Clara*, *First National Bank of Boston*, *Austin*, *Citizens United*, and any other case in which corporate personhood was addressed would have been irrelevant. In addition, it is obvious that the issue of corporate expenditures towards the political process would also have been appropriately addressed (e.g., regulated or eliminated).

In conclusion, what is most troubling is the fact that *We the People* have come to depend on and rely upon the Court to uphold the Constitution and follow the law (e.g., precedents). Contrary to widely held beliefs of the political elite (e.g., congress, justices, and presidents), *We the People* are capable of reading and comprehending legal decisions once they are translated into plain, non-technical language as compared to legal hyperbole. Alexander Hamilton personified such a belief when he stated "The people are turbulent and changing; they seldom judge or determine right. Give therefore to the first class a distinct, permanent share in the government." In the case of *Citizens United*, it is quite apparent that the Court erred in its judgment while making a simple case into a lengthy oration that attempts to equate the anatomy of an abstract to the physiology of a human being.

THE MORE THINGS CHANGE, THE MORE THEY REMAIN THE SAME

In recent years, the decisions rendered by the Supreme Court have called into question its duty and responsibility as guardian and interpreter of the Constitution. In essence, the legitimacy of the Court has been jeopardized by partisan politics, legislating from the bench, ignoring precedent, and failing to conduct thorough Constitutional and historical research to name a few. Ironically, the Justices (throughout the Court's history) have no one to blame but themselves. However, they continually fail to recognize their own errors in judgment and place the culpability primarily on outside influences.

In the aftermath of Roe v. Wade being overturned, Chief Justice John Roberts expressed his concerns regarding the public's perception of the Court by stating:

"If the court doesn't retain its legitimate function of interpreting the constitution, I'm not sure who would take up that mantle. You don't want the political branches telling you what the law is, and you don't want public opinion to be the guide about what the appropriate decision is." [[lxxxv]]

Justice Neil Gorsuch added:

> *"Improper efforts to influence judicial decision-making, from whatever side, from whomever, are a threat to the judicial decision-making process."* [[lxxxvi]]

Nine months earlier, at a speech at the University of Louisville's McConnell Center, Justice Amy Coney Barrett explained that:

> *"My goal today is to convince you that this court is not comprised of a bunch of partisan hacks."* [[lxxxvii]]

She further elaborated that the Court is defined by "judicial philosophies" instead of personal political views and that:

> *"Judicial philosophies are not the same as political parties."* [[lxxxviii]]

Like the rationale in *Roe*, the Constitution *"makes no express reference of* corporations." [[lxxxix]] The Court in *Santa Clara County v. Southern Pacific Railroad* was *"egregiously wrong and on a collision course with the Constitution from the day it was decided."* [[xc]] The authority to regulate corporations should immediately *"be returned to the people and their elected representatives."* [[xci]]

As previously illustrated, the decision in *Santa Clara County* was not only politically motivated, but it was also laced with corruption and conflicts of interest within the Court itself. In addition, prior court precedents, *Dartmouth College v. Woodward* and *Bank of Augusta v. Earle*, concluded that corporations were "an artificial being, invisible, intangible, and existing only in contemplation of the law."

In addition, and based upon the historical precedents of Edward Coke, William Blackstone, John Marshall, and Roger Taney, *Santa Clara County*, *First National Bank of Boston v. Bellotti* and *Citizens United v. Federal Election Commission* all should be overturned. Corporate law "possesses only those properties which the charter of its creation confers upon it" and "can have no legal existence out of the boundaries of the sovereignty by which it is created." [[xcii]] Simply stated, corporations are, and have always been, a state's matter.

Another example of the Court's literary license to Constitutional interpretation came in *Buckley v. Valeo* when it ruled that money was equivalent to speech. The original intent of the 1st Amendment was to protect political speech of an individual without fearing censorship, penalties, or retaliation from the government. Prior to *Buckley*, speech consisted of the spoken or written word, marches, protests, and other means of communication. The irony of the rationale given by the Justices in their decision was that they could not phantom the notion that expressing one's political views could be made without the expenditure of money, yet they somehow could equate an inanimate tangible object to speech. At least three errors in judgment are evident in their decision-making process. First, the Justices did not conduct thorough research regarding the concept of earned and free media. Second, they failed to identify that both speech and money are separate commodities. Third, money was a medium of exchange in colonial America during the ratification process, yet interestingly, the Founders chose not to include it in the 1st Amendment as a form of speech.

The data presented within has clearly illustrated that the Supreme Court and its Justices have a history of partisanship and political influence. To believe otherwise is disingenuous at best. It starts with the "grooming" of Justices, then works its way to the President nominating a candidate who possesses a specific ideology for a vacancy on the Court. The nomination and appointment of John Marshall is a textbook example of the politics at play.

In 1800, Congress eliminated a vacant seat from the Court to prevent President Thomas Jefferson from filling an opening simply because he was from the opposing political party. [[xciii]]

In 1937, President Franklin Delano Roosevelt sought to pass the Judicial Procedures Reform Bill that was to permit him to appoint an additional six Justices to the Court to move his political agenda forward. [[xciv]]

Not to mention the partisan paths several of the current Justices followed on their way to the Court. For example, Chief Justice Roberts worked in the administrations of Presidents Ronald Reagan and George H.W. Bush, Justice Elena Kagan under President Bill Clinton, and Justices Neil Gorsuch and Brett Kavanaugh under President George W. Bush.

If partisanship and political influence were absent from the Court, there would be a much greater concerted effort by the Justices to discover the original intent of the Founders. Instead, however, there has been a consistent dose of division inherently prescribed by the nature of politics itself. Whether liberal or conservative, federalist or anti-federalist, the Justices are not raised in a vacuum. Their biases and prejudices are evident from the onset of a case being heard. As if in a criminal case, each side attempts to persuade the other that their interpretation of the Constitution is correct. Their error in judgement lies in the fact that determining the constitutionality of an issue should never be a win or lose supposition. The consequences of their decisions have a profound impact on society and should be rendered with care, caution, and certainty. Not based upon partisanship or political influence.

As it pertains to the Constitution itself, the Court and its Justices appear to operate with the mindset that the document is static in stature, yet dynamic to interpretation. Quite the contrary. The Constitution is dynamic in size, but static in meaning. Rather than simply declaring an issue unconstitutional, remanding it back to Congress for rework, or suggesting an amendment, the Justices seem compelled to bend, stretch, or manipulate the original context and intent of the Founders to fit contemporary issues.

Although heralded by the legal profession, Marshall's decision and subsequent comment in Marbury that:

> *"It is emphatically the province and duty of the Judicial Department [the judicial branch] to say what the law is."*

has done irrevocable harm to the democratic republic. It was a deliberate act to assert the Court's authority over the executive and legislative branches, which has also transcended to the people. The Founders never intended for one branch of the government to be superior to the other two, let alone be untouchable. In Federalist 78, Alexander Hamilton states that the Justices ought to be governed by the people rather than the legislature. Furthermore, he proclaims that:

> *"They ought to regulate their decisions by the fundamental laws, rather than by those which are not fundamental."*

The Constitution being the fundamental law that is derived from "the intention of the people to the intention of their agents." According to Hamilton, the power of the people is superior to the judiciary and judicial review was to ensure that the will of the people was supreme. [[xcv]] The unfortunate reality, however, is that the Court since *Marbury* has incrementally replaced the intentions of the people, who through their state representatives ratified the Constitution, with Justices who have hijacked the Founders original intent and replaced it with their own social, economic, or political ambitions.

The legal community (e.g., judges, lawyers, and scholars) often contends that uncovering the original meaning of the Founders is extremely difficult, and therefore necessitates interpretation. Such an argument is nothing more than courtroom chicanery to create reasonable doubt as to the intentions of the people, through their representatives, who ratified the Constitution. There are copious amounts of historical documents (e.g., Federalist and Anti-Federalist papers, personal letters, recorded debates, etc.) readily available that contain the answers. The ratification is proof that, at a minimum, a consensus of meaning and understanding of the text was reached. If there was not, the Constitution would not have been signed and ratified.

Whether it's arrogance, ego, or lack of faith in humanity, there appears to be a great deal of elitism within the legal and political realm dating back to the founding of the nation. In terms of the mindset of the Supreme Court since *Marbury* through present day, Gouverneur Morris offers his take that the necessity of an independent judiciary is:

". . . to save the people from their most dangerous enemy, themselves."

Furthermore, the belief that the text within the Constitution, which is *the supreme Law of the Land*, is not a law until the Supreme Court declares it to be law via judicial review is not only an absurdity but an affront to the citizenry.

It cannot go without saying that the executive and legislative branches have been derelict in their duties and responsibilities by passing along difficult issues on to the courts for decisions on constitutionality. However, as guardians of the Constitution, the Justices should adhere to their job description, which consists of:

- Not being political
- Remaining neutral
- Only ruling on the constitutionality of the matter at hand
- Not legislating from the bench
- Keeping emotions in check
- Conducting thorough research

In conclusion, the Court has failed to be an efficient and effective guardian of the Constitution. By their own decisions, the Justices have jeopardized the integrity of the Court. Through the years, they have become so entrenched in their own agendas (e.g., leaving a mark on history) that they cannot see the forest through the trees. Documented history clearly illustrates that the Court is a political entity, and the fault lies within. There was a reason why the Founders made the three branches of government equal. It is part of the system of checks and balances. However, the *Marbury* decision tilted the balance of power in favor of the judiciary, which is accountable to no one. The result is precisely what Brutus (believed to be Robert Yates) wrote in The Power of the Judiciary (Part 2) on January 31, 1788, and Thomas Jefferson wrote William Charles Jarvis in 1820, respectively:

> *"It is, moreover, of great importance, to examine with care the nature and extent of the judicial power, because those who are to be vested with it, are to be placed in a situation altogether unprecedented in a free country. They are to be rendered totally independent, both of the people and the legislature, both with respect to their offices and salaries. No errors they may commit can be corrected by any power above them, if any such power there be, nor can they be removed from office for making ever so many erroneous adjudications."*

> *"You seem ... to consider the judges as the ultimate arbiters of all constitutional questions; a very dangerous doctrine indeed, and one which would place us under the despotism of an oligarchy. Our judges are as honest as other men, and not more so. They have, with others, the same passions for party, for power, and the privilege of their corps.... Their power [is] the more dangerous as they are in office for life, and not responsible, as the other functionaries are, to the elective control. The Constitution has erected no such single tribunal, knowing that to whatever hands confided, with*

the corruptions of time and party, its members would become despots. It has more wisely made all the departments co-equal and co-sovereign within themselves.

When the legislative or executive functionaries act unconstitutionally, they are responsible to the people in their elective capacity. The exemption of the judges from that is quite dangerous enough. I know no safe depository of the ultimate powers of the society but the people themselves; and if we think them not enlightened enough to exercise their control with a wholesome discretion, the remedy is not to take it from them but to inform their discretion by education. This is the true corrective of abuses of Constitutional power."

APPENDIX

[i] https://www.supremecourt.gov/about/constitutional.aspx

[ii] ibid

[iii] https://constitution.congress.gov/browse/essay/intro.7-1/ALDE_00001302/

[iv] https://nccs.net/blogs/articles/the-federal-judiciary-guardian-or-destroyer

[v] https://famguardian.org/Subjects/Politics/ThomasJefferson/jeff1020.htm

[vi] https://constitution.congress.gov/browse/essay/intro.7-3/ALDE_00001304/

[vii] https://onlinelibrary.wiley.com/doi/abs/10.1111/j.1540-5818.2006.00130.x

[viii] https://patch.com/massachusetts/attleboro/bp--thomas-jefferson-and-john-marshall-founding-fathe0e112006ee

[ix] https://www.history.com/news/supreme-court-power-john-marshall

[x] ibid

[xi] https://reason.com/2017/05/15/the-birth-of-the-living-constitution/

[xii] https://www.wonderopolis.org/wonder/who-invented-money#:~text=Sometimes%20people%20%20couldn't%20agree,items%20used%20by%20almost%20everyone

[xiii] https://www.thoughtco.com/the-double-

coincidence-of-wants-defintion-1147998

[xiv] https://www.wonderopolis.org/wonder/who-invented-money#:text=Sometimes%20people%20%couldn't%20agree,items%20used%20by%20almost%20everyone.

[xv] https://www.investopedia.com/terms/m/money.asp

[xvi] https://www.stlouisfed.org/education/economic-lowdown-podcast-series/episode-9-functions-of-money#:~:text=To%20summarize%2C%20money%20has%20taken,account%2C%20and%20medium%20of%20exchange.

[xvii] https://www.fec.gov/legal-resources/court-cases/buckley-v-valeo/

[xviii] ibid

[xix] ibid

[xx] ibid

[xxi] https://www.nytimes.com/2016/03/16/upshot/measuring-donald-trumps-mammoth-advantage-in-free-media.html

[xxii] ibid

[xxiii] https://www.fec.gov/introduction-campaign-finance/understanding-ways-support-federal-candidates/presidential-elections/public-funding-presidential-elections/#:~:text=Under%20the%20presidential%20public%20funding,the%20primary%20and%20general%20elections.

[xxiv] https://www.washingtonpost.com/news/post-politics/wp/2016/12/09/the-six-donors-trump-appointed-to-his-administration-gave-almost-12-million-with-their-families-to-his-campaign-and-the-party

[xxv] https://www.politico.com/story/2011/06/obama-donors-net-government-jobs-056993

[xxvi] ibid
[xxvii] ibid
[xxviii] https://www.independent.org/news/article.asp?id=448
[xxix] https://www.law.cornell.edu/wex/bribery#:~:text=Overview,a%20public%20or%20legal%20duty
[xxx] https://www.accountingtools.com/articles/corporation-advantages-and-disadvantages.html
[xxxi] https://news.law.fordham.edu/jcfl/2018/11/18/a-brief-history-of-the-corporate-form-and-why-it-matters/
[xxxii] ibid
[xxxiii] ibid
[xxxiv] https://www.amacad.org/publication/american-corporation
[xxxv] https://www.stamfordadvocate.com/local/article/Angela-Carella-Founding-fathers-worried-about-3628729.php
[xxxvi] ibid
[xxxvii] ibid
[xxxviii] https://www.americanbar.org/groups/crsj/publications/human_rights_magazine_home/we-the-people/we-the-people-corporations/
[xxxix] https://news.law.fordham.edu/jcfl/2018/11/18/a-brief-history-of-the-corporate-form-and-why-it-matters/
[xl] ibid
[xli] ibid
[xlii] https://newint.org/features/2002/07/05/history#:~:text=Prior%20to%20the%2017th%20century,these%20was%20punishable%20by%20law.

[xliii] https://ballotpedia.org/Santa_Clara_County_v._Southern_Pacific_Railroad_Company

[xliv] https://www.encyclopedia.com/law/encyclopedias-almanacs-transcripts-and-maps/santa-clara-county-v-southern-pacific-railroad-company

[xlv] ibid

[xlvi] https://libguides.eku.edu/c.php?g=844563&p=6049971

[xlvii] https://supreme.justia.com/cases/federal/us/118/394/#tab-opinion-1911273

[xlviii] ibid

[xlix] ibid

[l] https://www.theatlantic.com/business/archive/2018/03/corporations-people-adam-winkler/554852/

[li] ibid

[lii] https://truthout.org/articles/unequal-protection-the-deciding-moment/#3

[liii] https://www.infoplease.com/history/us/ulysses-s-grant-credit-mobilier-the-whiskey-ring

[liv] https://www.oyez.org/justices/morrison_r_waite and https://ballotpedia.org/Morrison_Waite

[lv] https://truthout.org/articles/unequal-protection-the-deciding-moment/#3

[lvi] https://slate.com/news-and-politics/2014/03/hobby-lobby-and-corporate-personhood-heres-the-real-history-of-corporate-rights-in-america.html

[lvii] https://www.americanbar.org/groups/crsj/publications/human_rights_magazine_home/we-the-people/we-the-people-corporations/

[lviii] https://truthout.org/articles/unequal-protection-the-deciding-moment/#3

[lix] https://www.fec.gov/legal-resources/court-cases/first-national-bank-of-boston-v-bellotti/

[lx] ibid

[lxi] ibid

[lxii] https://supreme.justia.com/cases/federal/us/435/765/#tab-opinion-1952583

[lxiii] https://www.fec.gov/legal-resources/court-cases/first-national-bank-of-boston-v-bellotti/

[lxiv] ibid

[lxv] ibid

[lxvi] ibid

[lxvii] ibid

[lxviii] ibid

[lxix] A. Bradford, Sentiments on the Liberty of the Press, in L. Levy, Freedom of the Press from Zenger to Jefferson 41-42 (1966) (emphasis deleted) (first published in Bradford's The American Weekly Mercury, a Philadelphia newspaper, Apr. 25, 1734).

[lxx] https://lonang.com/library/reference/blackstone-commentaries-law-england/bla-118/

[lxxi] https://tile.loc.gov/storage-services/service/ll/usrep/usrep435/usrep435765/usrep435765.pdf

[lxxii] ibid

[lxxiii] ibid

[lxxiv] ibid

[lxxv] ibid

[lxxvi] https://www.fec.gov/legal-resources/court-cases/austin-v-michigan-state-chamber-of-commerce/

[lxxvii] https://www.fec.gov/resources/legal-resources/litigation/cu_sc08_opinion.pdf

[lxxviii] https://www.lexisnexis.com/community/casebrief/p/casebrief-mcconnell-v-fec

[lxxix] ibid
[lxxx] https://www.fec.gov/resources/legal-resources/litigation/cu_sc08_opinion.pdf
[lxxxi] ibid
[lxxxii] ibid
[lxxxiii] https://www.fec.gov/resources/legal-resources/litigation/cu_sc08_opinion.pdf
[lxxxiv] https://www.law.cornell.edu/wex/stare_decisis
[lxxxv] https://apnews.com/article/abortion-us-supreme-court-denver-public-opinion-john-roberts-6921c22df48b105cdff5fabdc6c459bb
[lxxxvi] ibid
[lxxxvii] https://www.cnn.com/2021/09/13/politics/amy-coney-barrett-supreme-court-not-partisan/index.html
[lxxxviii] ibid
[lxxxix] https://www.supremecourt.gov/opinions/21pdf/19-1392_6j37.pdf
[xc] ibid
[xci] ibid
[xcii] https://www.lexisnexis.com/community/casebrief/p/casebrief-trs-of-dartmouth-coll-v-woodward
[xciii] https://www.politico.com/news/magazine/2022/01/28/supreme-court-is-political-always-has-been-00003224
[xciv] https://sutherlandinstitute.org/congress-history-of-messing-with-supreme-court-size/
[xcv] https://www.supremecourt.gov/about/constitutional.aspx

www.ingramcontent.com/pod-product-compliance
Lightning Source LLC
Chambersburg PA
CBHW071145240526
45465CB00024BA/1783